PENPALS *for* Handwriting

Year 5 Practice Book (9-10 years)

By **Gill Budgell & Kate Ru**

Supported by the
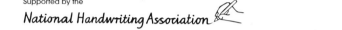
National Handwriting Association
Promoting good practice

T0268539

Contents

Term 1

1 **Introducing sloped writing in letter families** ... 2
2 **Practising sloped writing: diagonal join to ascender:** *th, sh, nb, nd, ht, st* ... 3
3 **Practising sloped writing: diagonal join, no ascender:** *ai, ay, kn, er, ie, en* ... 4
4 **Practising sloped writing: diagonal join to an anticlockwise letter:** *ac, sc, bo, da, ea, ho* ... 5
5 **Practising sloped writing: horizontal join to ascender:** *wh, wl, oh, ol, of, ob* ... 6
6 **Practising sloped writing: horizontal join, no ascender:** *oi, oy, ou, op, ve* ... 7
7 **Practising sloped writing: horizontal join to an anticlockwise letter:** *oo, oa, wa, wo, va, vo* ... 8
8 **Practising sloped writing: joining from** *r: ra, re, ri, ro, ru* ... 9
9 **Practising sloped writing: joining from** *s: sh, su, sc, sl, sw, sp* ... 10
10 **End-of-term check** ... 11

Term 2

11 **Practising sloped writing: proportion – joining from** *f* **to ascender:** *fl, ft* ... 12
12 **Practising sloped writing: size – joining from** *f*, **no ascender:** *fa, fe, fi, fo, fu* ... 13
13 **Different styles for different purposes: writing a paragraph** ... 14
14 **Practising sloped writing: speed:** *ff* ... 15

15 **Practising sloped writing: speed and legibility:** *rr* ... 16
16 **Practising sloped writing: size, proportion and spacing:** *ss* ... 17
17 **Practising sloped writing: building speed:** *qu* ... 18
18 **Different styles for different purposes: decorative alphabets** ... 19
19 **Different styles for different purposes** ... 20
20 **End-of-term check** ... 21

Term 3

21 **Sloped writing: proportion: joining** *p* **and** *b* **to ascenders:** *ph, pl, bl* ... 22
22 **Handwriting for different purposes: joining from** *p* **and** *b*, **no ascender:** *bu, bi, pe, pu, pi, pr* ... 23
23 **Practising sloped writing: parallel downstrokes:** *bb, pp* ... 24
24 **Practising sloped writing: all double letters** ... 25
25 **Practising sloped writing for speed:** *tial, cial* ... 26
26 **Practising sloped writing for fluency** ... 27
27 **Personal style** ... 28
28 **Handwriting for different purposes: print alphabet** ... 29
29 **Assessments** ... 30
30 **Capitals** ... 32

Lower-case and capital alphabet

CAMBRIDGE UNIVERSITY PRESS

Practise the letters. Now write each letter with
a slope that is comfortable and speedy for you.

l i t u j y

r b n h m k p

c a d o s g q e f

v w x z

Write your name in sloped writing.

Speeding up
Rewrite at least three times
at an increasing speed:

We use a slope
to increase
fluency and speed.

Check:
- the slope of your handwriting.

Find two letters to tick and two to improve.
Rewrite them.

Read and write
the words.

slope

slope

alphabet

alphabet

angle

angle

Practise the joins. Now write each join with a slope that is comfortable and speedy for you.

th   sh   nb   nd   ht   st

th   sh   nb   nd   ht   st

Write the rhyme to practise your slope.

Whether the weather be cold
Or whether the weather be hot,
We'll weather the weather
Whatever the weather,
Whether we like it or not.

Anonymous

Practise the pattern.

Check:
- the slope of your handwriting
- the joins to ascenders.

Find two words to tick and two to improve.
Rewrite them.

Read and write the words.

storm

storm

lightning

lightning

sunshine

sunshine

3

Practise the joins. Now write each join with a slope that is comfortable and speedy for you.

ai   ay   kn   er   ie   en

ai   ay   kn   er   ie   en

Write the text to practise your slope.

Do you know "The Rime of the Ancient Mariner", by Samuel Taylor Coleridge?

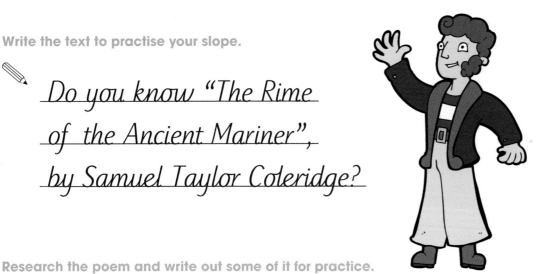

Research the poem and write out some of it for practice.

Practise the pattern.

Check:
- the slope of your handwriting
- the joins to letters with no ascenders.

Find two words to tick and two to improve.
Rewrite them.

4

Read and write the words.

poem

poem

recite

recite

rhyme

rhyme

Practise the joins. Now write each join with a slope that is comfortable and speedy for you.

ac   sc   bo   da   ea   ho

ac   sc   bo   da   ea   ho

Join each of Set 1 letters to at least two of the Set 2 letters.

Set 1	Set 2	Example
a b c d e	*a c d*	*aa ad ba bc*
h i k l m	*g o q*	
n p q s t u	*s*	

How many combinations can you make?

Practise the pattern.

Check:
- the slope of your handwriting
- the diagonal join.

Find two words to tick and two to improve. Rewrite them.

Read and write the words.

patterns

patterns

vowels

vowels

combinations

combinations

Practise the joins. Now write each join with a slope that is comfortable and speedy for you.

wh   wl   oh   ol   of   ob

wh   wl   oh   ol   of   ob

Write a question web. You might not use your best handwriting for this web, but make sure your writing is legible.

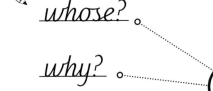

whose?   who?   whether?

why?   why?

which?   when?

wh

Choose a topic. Write it in the centre. Write a question about your topic using each word.

Practise the pattern.

Check:
- the slope of your handwriting
- the joins to ascenders.

Find two words to tick and two to improve.
Rewrite them.

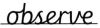

Read and write the words.

observe

observe

symbol

symbol

knowledge

knowledge

6

Practise the joins. Now write each join with a slope that is comfortable and speedy for you.

oi   oy   ou   op   ve

oi   oy   ou   op   ve

Write the text.

I have found an old joke:
Which type of pop group did
The Young Mummies join?
A boy bandage!

Write your own joke.

Speeding up
Rewrite at least three times at an increasing speed:

That joke is not funny

Check:
- the slope of your handwriting
- the horizontal joins.

Find two words to tick and two to improve.
Rewrite them.

Read and write the words.

have

have

love

love

found

found

7

Practise the joins. Now write each join with a slope that is comfortable and speedy for you.

oo   oa   wa   wo   va   vo

oo   oa   wa   wo   va   vo

Join each of Set 1 letters to at least two of Set 2 letters.

Set 1	Set 2	Example
ow	*a c d*	*oa oc od*
r v	*g o q*	
f	*s*	

How many combinations can you make?

Speeding up
Rewrite at least three times
at an increasing speed:

*Keep letters clear
when writing
at speed.*

Check:
- the slope of your handwriting
- the horizontal joins.

Find two joins to tick and two to improve.
Rewrite them.

Read and write
the words.

footprints

footprints

wandering

wandering

vagabond

vagabond

Practise the joins. Now write each join with a slope that is comfortable
and speedy for you.

ra   re   ri   ro   ru

ra   re   ri   ro   ru

Write the word list in joined, sloped writing. Keep the vowels in a line.

marvellous
different
describe
controversy
bruise

Use a quick, but legible, handwriting to plan your own word list like this,
showing the vowels in a line.

Practise the pattern.

Check:
- the slope of your joins
- your joins from *r*.
Find two words to tick and two to improve.
Rewrite them.

Read and write
the words.

random

require

ridiculous

round

ruin

very

Practise the joins. Now write each join with a slope that is comfortable and speedy for you.

sh   su   sc   sl   sw   sp

sh   su   sc   sl   sw   sp

Write the sentence in joined, sloped writing.

She stared at her shiny shuffling shoes and screamed.

Write at least three scary sentences using these words.
Use a sloped, fluent handwriting style.

shiver	soldier	shriek	snake
slither	astronaut	slide	skeleton
scratch	ghost	scar	stare

Speeding up
Rewrite at least three times
at an increasing speed:

Keep letters the
correct size when
speeding up

Add prefixes or suffixes to change
the words if you need to.

Check:
- the slope of your joins
- your joins from *s*.

Find two words to tick and two to improve.
Rewrite them.

strange

island

invisible

suspicious

fantasy

science fiction

Write the text out neatly but speedily. Use a slope that is comfortable for you.

The pterygotus, which was also known as the 'water scorpion', was one of the first land creatures. It lived about 300 million years ago and it could be up to 2 metres long.

Write a new heading for this text in your own handwriting style.

Speeding up
Rewrite at least three times at an increasing speed:

Keep the correct letter and word spacing when speeding up

Write one benefit of sloped writing.
Write one disadvantage of it.
Write a handwriting target for yourself.

Read and write the words.

history

pre-historic

vertebrate

geology

museums

researchers

Practise the joins.

fl   fl   ft   ft

Write the text.

Tiger and Fire
In the beginning of the world, it was Tiger
who owned the fire of the world. The fire
flared as the flames flickered and flashed
like fireflies. He fed it often so that the gift
of fire flourished.

Speeding up
Rewrite at least three times
at an increasing speed:

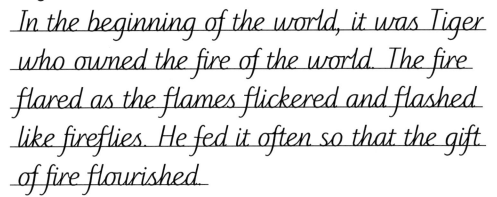

Keep letters in
the correct letter
proportions when
speeding up.

Check:
- the slope of the join to ascenders
- the height of the *f* in relation to the *l* and *t*.
Find two words to tick and two to improve.
Rewrite them.

Read and write
the words.

fable

soften

forest

thereafter

swiftness

inflection

Practise the joins.

fa   fe   fi   fo   fu

Write the heading. Write the text.

Fish fact file
* fish have different numbers and kinds of fins
* freshwater fish may live in fast-moving rivers
* saltwater fish may live on coral reefs

Read and write
the words.

five

fifteen

fifty

Speeding up
Rewrite at least three times
at an increasing speed:

Regular letter
sizing makes
writing easier
to read.

Check:
- the comparative size of all the f joins
  you have written
- your slope.

Find two words to tick and two to improve.
Rewrite them.

fantastic

information

future

13

Write a paragraph about these facts.

Bat facts

- _warm blooded_
- _only mammals able to fly_
- _babies called 'pups'_
- _have fur_
- _have thumb and 4 very long fingers_
- _many kinds; about 1,000 species_
- _feed at night_
- _hang upside down sleeping in
  a 'roost' in the day_

Read and write the words.

dashes

commas

brackets

clause

paragraph

parenthesis

Practise the pattern.

Check:
- the spacing of your letters and words
- your slope.

Find two words to tick and two to improve.
Rewrite them.

Practise the joins.

ff ff ff ff ff ff

Write these words in alphabetical order.

baffled   *ruffled*

scuffle   *scruffy*

sniffled   *snuffled*

snuffle   *truffle*

Speeding up
Rewrite at least three times
at an increasing speed:

*The scruffy thing
snuffled and
scuffled away*

Check:
- the ascenders of ff are the same
  height, and the descenders are equal *ff*
- the slope.

Find two words to tick and two to improve.
Rewrite them.

Read and write
the words.

duffle

handcuff

official

difficult

different

sufficient

Practise the join.

   *rr   rr   rr   rr   rr*

Write out the speech bubbles.

I'm arranging the carrots.

*Make way for
my wheelbarrow.*

*Tasty berries and
fresh cherries!*

purr, purr

Hurry! Hurry!

Add another speech bubble featuring *rr* words.

Speeding up
Rewrite at least three times
at an increasing speed:

*Harry left in a
hurry with a flurry*

Check:
- the joined *rr*s are the same size
- the layout of your writing
- legibility.

Find two words to tick and two to improve.
Rewrite them.

Read and write
the words.

flurry

borrow

narrow

horrible

barrier

irregular

Practise the join.

 *ss   ss   ss   ss   ss   ss*

Write out the poster.

Read and write
the words.

Class Chess Club

We have assorted boards to choose from.
Impressive players.
Discuss key moves and assist others.

no experience necessary

success is possible

message

process

session

assistance

classic

successful

Practise the pattern.

Check:
- the joined *ss* are the same size and
  height as each other
- your slope.

Find two words to tick and two to improve.
Rewrite them.

Practise the joins.

qu qu qu qu qu

Write the following paragraph using words from the box below.

Many   occur near the   .
Earthquake response teams
specialist training and   . They are
highly   and they must follow a
strict   of events in their responses.

equator	*equipment*	*qualified*
require	*earthquakes*	*sequence*

Speeding up
Rewrite at least three times
at an increasing speed:

Queue quietly
with questions

Check:
- the spacing between the *q* and the *u*
- your slope.

Find two words to tick and two to improve.
Rewrite them.

Read and write the words.

quest

unique

enquire

liquid

aqua

frequently

Try creating your own capital letter fonts that you might use on posters or invitations.

Here are some ideas to inspire you. Try each and then create some of your own.

Read and write the words.

QRST   UVWX   YZ   You choose!

font

text

letter

height

width

spacing

Speeding up
Rewrite at least three times at an increasing speed:

Choose the right
handwriting style
for the purpose.

Check:
- sizing, spacing and proportion of each set of letters is consistent.

Find two letters to tick and two to improve.
Rewrite them.

Write the months of the year in sloped, joined writing. Then write them in upright print writing.

January   January   *July*

February   *August*

March   *September*

April   *October*

May   *November*

June   *December*

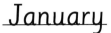

month

calendar

weekly

planner

diary

electronic

Speeding up
Rewrite at least three times at an increasing speed:

different styles of
handwriting for
different purposes

Check:
- your slope
- your print letters
- your capitals.

Find two words to tick and two to improve.
Rewrite them.

20

Write the text. Answer each question with true or false.

The fact is that information technology is very exciting, but digital devices and games require us to follow precise instructions in a sequence if we are to be effective

Write out the statements that are true.

1. I can write notes in scruffy handwriting if it is legible.
2. The best handwriting for a sign or label is joined and sloped.
3. Print alphabet has no exit flicks and letters are upright.
4. Sloped writing should be leaning backwards.
5. A slope may be less useful for left-handed writers.
6. Uneven spacing of letters or words is tricky to read.
7. It doesn't matter if two letters bump together.
8. Short ascenders make letters confusing e.g. is it n or h?
9. Long descenders can get mixed up with the letters on the line above.

Give yourself a mark out of 10 for the neatness of your handwriting.

/10

Work with a partner to check you have identified the rules that are true.

Read and write the words.

systems

programs

input

algorithms

networks

output

Practise the joins.

ph   ph   pl   pl   bl   bl

Write and continue the short story. Focus on parallel, sloped, downward strokes.

The pharaoh put a blanket on the elephant's back and rode triumphantly to the peoples' applause. They blew whistles and cheered to show their complete pleasure in his courage. The elephant, although a simple beast...

Continue using as many *ph*, *pl* and *bl* words as you can.

Speeding up
Rewrite at least three times
at an increasing speed:

The pharaoh put a blanket on the elephant's back.

Check:
- your slope
- the parallel lines of *p, b, h, l.*

Find two words to tick and two to improve.
Rewrite them.

Read and write
the words.

complete

complain

plough

autobiography

physical

valuable

Practise the joins.

 *bu   bi   pe   pu   pi   pr*

Write a list of each animal and its preferred food type.

 *chimpanzee*   *bamboo*
panda   *impala*
hippopotamus   *seals*
polar bears   *seeds and berries*
leopard   *bananas*
baboon   *grass plants*

What sort of handwriting did you use for this list?

Speeding up
Rewrite at least three times
at an increasing speed:

Quick but legible
writing is fine for
notes and lists.

Check:
- that your list is neatly set out
- that your list is legible
- your joins from *p* and *b*
- you included a break at *z* in chimpanzee.

Find two words to tick and two to improve.
Rewrite them.

Read and write the words.

parakeet

especially

panther

humpback whale

punctuation

binoculars

Practise the joins.

 *bb   bb   bb   pp   pp   pp*

Write the words. Add, remove or replace prefixes to make words with the opposite meaning.

bb or *pp* word	Opposite
unabbreviated	_____
disapply	_____
appropriate	_____
approve	_____
reappear	_____
appealing	_____

Speeding up
Rewrite at least three times at an increasing speed:

It disappeared,
then reappeared
with a wobble,
and we clapped.

Add at least two more *bb, pp* words to the list.

Check:
- how parallel your ascenders and descenders are for *p* and *b*
- your slope.

Find two words to tick and two to improve.
Rewrite them.

Read and write the words.

equipped

wobble

clapped

approve

rubbish

supplementary

Practise the joins.

bb cc ff gg ll mm
oo pp rr ss tt zz

Write the words with their missing double letters.
Use all of the above examples at least once.

1. co___led

2. a___o___odate

3. a___re___ive

4. a___ached

5. marve___ous

6. su___icient

7. mu___le

8. emba___a___ed

9. o___ortunity

10. stu___orn

11. ba___n

12. whi___ed

Speeding up
Rewrite at least three times
at an increasing speed:

Marvellous, whizzy
communication.

Check:
- size
- spacing
- proportion.

Find two words to tick and two to improve.
Rewrite them.

Read and write the words.

agree

harass

communicate

accompany

possession

dissatisfied

Practise the joins.

tial   tial   cial   cial

Write this text at speed. Time it.

This is an official TV commercial.
Torrential rain is initially expected
on Monday and there is potential for snow.
Take special care when travelling.

Now assess it and try again to improve your handwriting and speed.

Practise the pattern.

Check:
- your slope
- the joins *tial* and *cial*
- capital letters
- legibility of your writing at speed.

Find two words to tick and two to improve.
Rewrite them.

Read and write the words.

social

especially

essential

partial

crucial

spatial

Practise the joins.

ie   ei   ie   ei   ie

es   ies   ves

Write each word in its plural form. Write quickly and smoothly.

vein   *variety*

belief   *dictionary*

loaf   *ceiling*

butterfly   *protein*

thief   *niece*

Now assess your writing and try again to improve your fluency.
Make your writing flow.

Practise the pattern.

Check:
- your slope
- the joins
- the loops of your *e* in *ie* or *ei*
- the legibility of your writing.

Find two words to tick and two to improve.
Rewrite them.

Read and write
the words.

sieve

veil

field

series

friends

kaleidoscope

27

Write this text in your own personal style. Write neatly and fluently.

Friends

I have a friend who likes knotting and one who likes knitting. I know others who enjoy climbing and boxing, and one who just knuckles down to hard work. But me? I like no hustle and bustle; it's thumbs up to an island life for me.

Practise the pattern.

Read and write the words.

castle

column

library

wrinkle

Autumn

asthma

Check:
- your personal style.
  How would you describe it?
- the joins
- the neatness of your writing at speed.

Find two words to tick and two to improve.
Rewrite them.

Practise the print alphabet.

a b c d e f g h i
j k l m n o p q r
s t u v w x y z

Print these words to label the diagram of the eye. Write a caption in print letters.

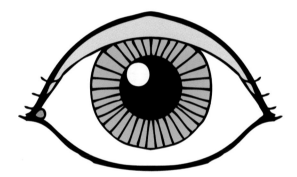

pupil
eyelid
tear duct
iris
eyelash

Speeding up
Rewrite at least three times
at an increasing speed:

different
handwriting for
different purposes

Check:
- your print letters
- spacing.
Find two words to tick and two to improve.
Rewrite them.

Read and write
the words.

label

diagram

clarity

printing

form filling

address

Write the jokes and answers in a joined, sloped handwriting style that is comfortable for you.
Then use the questions opposite to self-assess your handwriting.

Q. What reads and lives in an apple?
A. A bookworm.

Q. What's worse than finding a maggot in
your appple?
A. Finding half a maggot in your apple.

Write this word family. Add to it if you can.

joke limerick pun riddle
homophone homonym

Find your own maggot or worm joke to write out.

Use these questions to assess your own handwriting. Give yourself a mark out of 12.

1. Is your writing mostly joined when it should be?

2. Is the slope of your writing always the same?

3. Have you used print script correctly?

4. Are your descenders and ascenders parallel?

5. Are your descenders and ascenders clearly different from your x-height letters?

6. Is the spacing between letters and words even?

7. Are your x-height letters the same size?

8. Are your capital letters the same size?

9. Have you laid out the jokes neatly?

10. Did your hand move smoothly over the page as you wrote?

11. What are you most pleased with?

12. What do you need to improve?

Score /12

Write the rules for capital letters.

Read and write the words.

CAPITAL LETTERS

1. NEVER JOIN CAPITAL LETTERS.

2. MAKE THEM THE SAME HEIGHT
*   AS ASCENDERS.*

3. ALWAYS BEGIN AT THE TOP.

4. USE THEM TO BEGIN SENTENCES.

5. USE THEM FOR PERSONAL
*   NAMES AND TITLES.*

6. USE THEM FOR EMPHASIS.

RULES

POSTERS

PERSONAL NOUNS

EMPHASIS

CLARITY

VOLUME

Practise the pattern.

Check:
- capital letter formations for *E M K Y N*.
Find two words to tick and two to improve.
Rewrite them.